PAUL *and the* UNFRIENDLY TOWN

Acts 14:8-20 FOR CHILDREN

Written by Margaret Penner Toews

Illustrated by Obata Designs, Inc.,

Gordon Willman

CONCORDIA
Publishing House
St. Louis

ARCH Books

A mother in Lystra stood over her fire,
Smiling and stirring her stew.
She was telling her children a make-believe
  tale
That some people still thought was true.

"Long, long ago two gods came to Lystra,"
She said as they watched her stir.
"One was named Hermes, one was named
  Zeus,
But nobody guessed who they were!

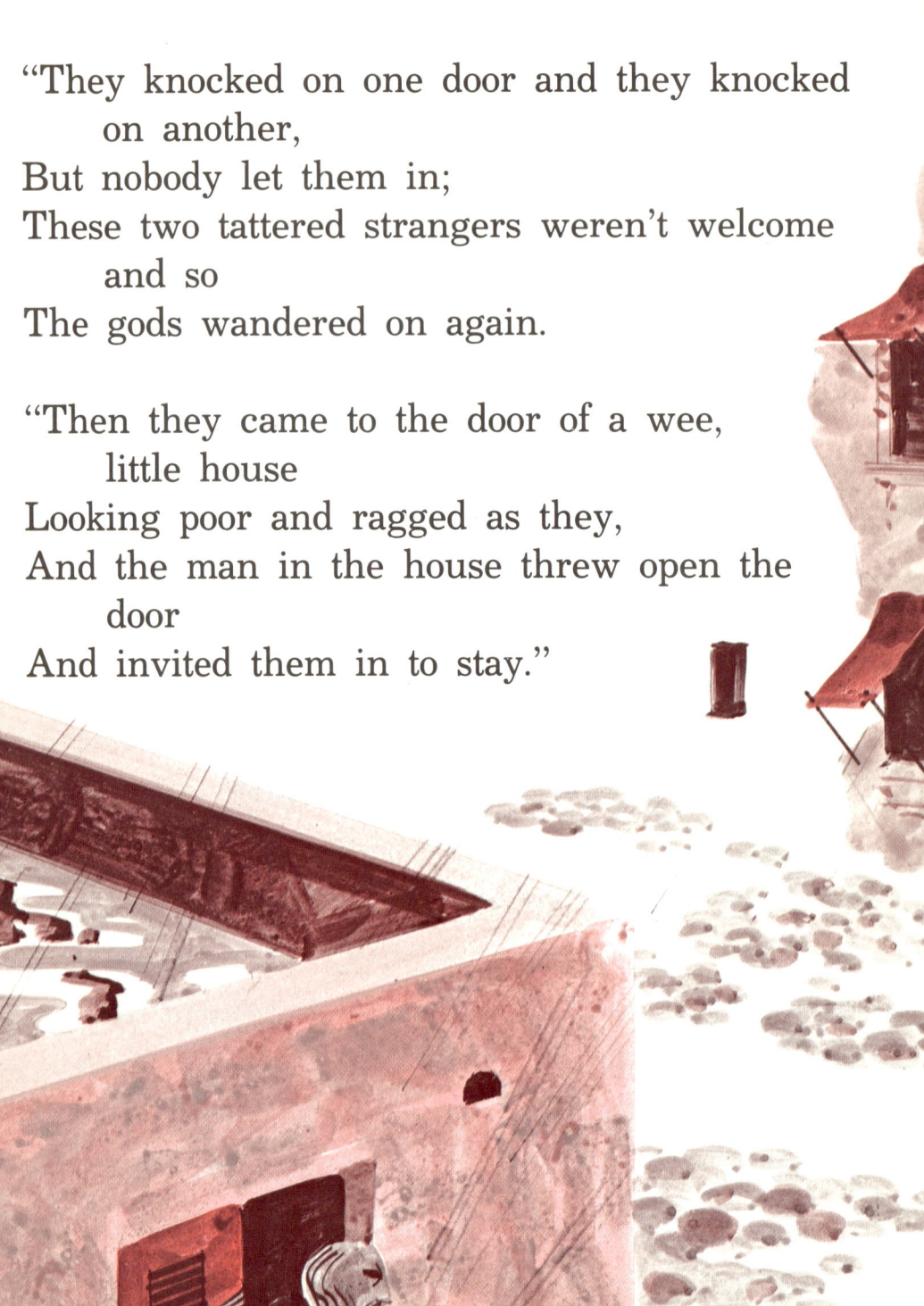

"They knocked on one door and they knocked
    on another,
But nobody let them in;
These two tattered strangers weren't welcome
    and so
The gods wandered on again.

"Then they came to the door of a wee,
    little house
Looking poor and ragged as they,
And the man in the house threw open the
    door
And invited them in to stay."

At this point in the story her Timmy
    and Artie
Shivered with utter delight.
"And what happened then?" they asked their
    mother.
"What did the gods do that night?"

"The gods turned that low, little house to
    gold,"
The mother in Lystra recited.

"It grew and it grew, and became *our temple!*"
"Ohhh!" said the children, excited.

"And the ones who had shooed those gods
   from their doors . . ."
(Tim and Artie listened agog),
"At once every one of those terrible folk
Turned into an ugly frog!

"Someday those gods will return to our
    temple.
So, Artie, you'd better be good;
And Timmie, you'd better be terribly nice!
Now eat, like good boys should."

The boys ate their soup and scampered away
To see what was new in town.
They ran to the market and up to the temple.
And guess what the two boys found!

It happened that Paul the apostle had come,
And Barnabas, too, that day.
They came to the gates of Lystra-town,
Took a look, and decided to stay.

They went to the temple of Hermes and Zeus,
Stood on the steps and said
To the people of Lystra, "We've come to
　　tell you
Of Someone who *rose from the dead!*"

Timmy and Artie gawked as they listened,
But most others just went on by.
These men didn't look important at all;
No doubt what they said was a lie.

Now meanwhile a hunched-up beggar,
Who'd been crippled since he was born,
Lay on the steps of the temple in Lystra,
Hot, unhappy, forlorn.

Timmie and Artie had seen him before.
They called him Crotchety Niel.
They saw him look up at Paul, who was
    telling
Of a God who was living and REAL.

Then Paul saw the beggar. "ARISE!" he
   called.
"IN THE NAME OF JESUS, ARISE!"
And the cripple's legs were suddenly straight.
He leaped with glad tears in his eyes.

Timmie and Artie and everyone else
Got excited and started to yell.
"What's this?" they exclaimed. "The gods
   have returned!
They made Niel's crippled legs well!"

Everyone hurried to tell their neighbors.
"Come and see! The gods have come down!"
People came crowding and swarming and
    shouting
From all over Lystra-town.

The priest of the temple hurriedly fetched
Some oxen and cartloads of flowers.
He piled up some stones for an altar
    and shouted,
"Come worship these gods of ours."

But suddenly Paul and Barnabas noticed
What all the ado was about.
Paul jumped on the pile of altar stones
And halted the priest with a shout.

"We are *not* gods! We are people like you!
Stop! Stop! Don't you dare sacrifice!
We did not heal this cripple of Lystra.
He was healed by the power of Christ."

The priest of Zeus dumped the flowers
And ordered the oxen muzzled.
"I don't understand it," he grumpily muttered.
All the people of Lystra were puzzled.

"Why do these gods not accept our honor?
Why do they turn down our praise?
What are they saying of good news and Jesus?
They've surely got us in a daze."

They looked again at Crotchety Niel,
Who still was leaping for joy.
They shook their heads and they looked
    at Paul
And felt just a little annoyed.

Some shuffled home and some stayed to listen,
Among them Artie and Tim.
What a wonderful God Paul was talking about!
They must tell their mother of Him!

Now a few days later some men came to
  Lystra,
And lo and behold, here was Paul!
They'd heard him before, and his story of
  Christ,
And they did not like him at all.

They whispered to all whom they met in the
    town,
"That Paul is a bad, bad man!
He's come here to turn you away from
    your gods.
Kill him as quick as you can!"

Zing! And somebody threw a stone.
Zing! It came right at Paul.
Thud, thump, thump, THUD! They threw the
    stones faster
And laughed when they saw him fall.

"He's dead!" they hooted, and dragged him out
Of the gates of Lystra that day;
And there by the side of the busy road
They let Paul the apostle lay.

Crotchety Niel and Timmy and Art
And some others watched him with dread.
Standing around him, they cried and cried,
So sorry their friend was dead.

But all of a sudden Paul opened his eyes
And looked up at each weeping friend.
"Don't cry," he said as he slowly rose.
"God has healed me. This isn't the end."